John Greenleaf Whittier

Saint Gregory's Guest, and Recent Poems

John Greenleaf Whittier

Saint Gregory's Guest, and Recent Poems

ISBN/EAN: 9783744712941

Printed in Europe, USA, Canada, Australia, Japan

Cover: Foto ©Thomas Meinert / pixelio.de

More available books at **www.hansebooks.com**

SAINT GREGORY'S GUEST
AND RECENT POEMS

BY

JOHN GREENLEAF WHITTIER

BOSTON AND NEW YORK
HOUGHTON, MIFFLIN AND COMPANY
The Riverside Press, Cambridge
1886

To

GEN. S. C. ARMSTRONG,

OF HAMPTON, VA.

Whose generous and self-denying labors for the elevation
of two races have enlisted my sympathies and
commanded my admiration,
I offer this Volume.

PREFATORY NOTE.

————◆————

I AM well aware that for the publication of a new volume of verse, when one is on the verge of fourscore, no adequate excuse can be offered. I frankly own that I know of no call for such an act of temerity. I have consulted nobody as to its expediency: and I cannot even adopt the doubtful apology of Bunyan: —

"Some said, John, print it ; others said not so :
Some said it might do good, others said no."

In taking upon myself the responsibility, I am influenced solely by a not unnatural wish to speak once more to those who have been pleased to listen to me heretofore, and to whom this little belated collection may not be without interest.　　　　　J. G. W.

CONTENTS.

SAINT GREGORY'S GUEST.

A TALE for Roman guides to tell
  To careless, sight-worn travellers still,
Who pause beside the narrow cell
  Of Gregory on the Cælian Hill.

One day before the monk's door came
  A beggar, stretching empty palms,
Fainting and fast-sick, in the name
  Of the Most Holy asking alms.

And the monk answered, " All I have
  In this poor cell of mine I give,
The silver cup my mother gave;
  In Christ's name take thou it, and live."

Years passed; and, called at last to bear
    The pastoral crook and keys of Rome,
The poor monk, in Saint Peter's chair,
    Sat the crowned lord of Christendom.

" Prepare a feast," Saint Gregory cried,
    " And let twelve beggars sit thereat."
The beggars came, and one beside,
    An unknown stranger, with them sat.

"I asked thee not," the Pontiff spake,
    " O stranger; but if need be thine,
I bid thee welcome, for the sake
    Of Him who is thy Lord and mine."

A grave, calm face the stranger raised,
    Like His who on Gennesaret trod,
Or His on whom the Chaldeans gazed,
    Whose form was as the Son of God.

" Know'st thou," he said, "thy gift of old?"
    And in the hand he lifted up

The Pontiff marvelled to behold
    Once more his mother's silver cup.

"Thy prayers and alms have risen, and bloom
    Sweetly among the flowers of heaven.
I am The Wonderful, through whom
    Whate'er thou askest shall be given."

He spake and vanished. Gregory fell
    With his twelve guests in mute accord
Prone on their faces, knowing well
    Their eyes of flesh had seen the Lord.

The old-time legend is not vain;
    Nor vain thy art, Verona's Paul,
Telling it o'er and o'er again
    On gray Vicenza's frescoed wall.

Still wheresoever pity shares
    Its bread with sorrow, want, and sin,
And love the beggar's feast prepares,
    The uninvited Guest comes in.

Unheard, because our ears are dull,
  Unseen, because our eyes are dim,
He walks our earth, The Wonderful,
  And all good deeds are done to Him.

REVELATION.

"And I went into the Vale of Beavor, and as I went I preached repentance to the people. And one morning, sitting by the fire, a great cloud came over me, and a temptation beset me. And it was said: *All things come by Nature;* and the Elements and the Stars came over me. And as I sat still and let it alone, a living hope arose in me, and a true Voice which said: *There is a living God who made all things.* And immediately the cloud and the temptation vanished, and Life rose over all, and my heart was glad and I praised the Living God."—*Journal of George Fox,* 1690.

STILL, as of old, in Beavor's Vale,
  O man of God! our hope and faith
The Elements and Stars assail,
  And the awed spirit holds its breath,
  Blown over by a wind of death.

Takes Nature thought for such as we,
  What place her human atom fills,
The weed-drift of her careless sea,
  The mist on her unheeding hills?
  What recks she of our helpless wills?

Strange god of Force, with fear, not love,
   Its trembling worshipper! Can prayer
Reach the shut ear of Fate, or move
   Unpitying Energy to spare?
   What doth the cosmic Vastness care?

In vain to this dread Unconcern
   For the All-Father's love we look;
In vain, in quest of it, we turn
   The storied leaves of Nature's book,
   The prints her rocky tablets took.

I pray for faith, I long to trust;
   I listen with my heart, and hear
A Voice without a sound: "Be just,
   Be true, be merciful, revere
   The Word within thee: God is near!

"A light to sky and earth unknown
   Pales all their lights: a mightier force
Than theirs the powers of Nature own,
   And, to its goal as at its source,
   His Spirit moves the Universe.

" Believe and trust. Through stars and suns,
   Through life and death, through soul and
      sense,
His wise, paternal purpose runs ;
   The darkness of His providence
   Is star-lit with benign intents."

O joy supreme ! I know the Voice,
   Like none beside on earth or sea ;
Yea, more, O soul of mine, rejoice,
   By all that He requires of me,
   I know what God himself must be.

No picture to my aid I call,
   I shape no image in my prayer ;
I only know in Him is all
   Of life, light, beauty, everywhere,
   Eternal Goodness here and there !

I know He is, and what He is,
   Whose one great purpose is the good
Of all. I rest my soul on His

Immortal Love and Fatherhood;
And trust Him, as His children should.

I fear no more.   The clouded face
  Of Nature smiles; through all her things
Of time and space and sense I trace
  The moving of the Spirit's wings,
  And hear the song of hope she sings.

ADJUSTMENT.

THE tree of Faith its bare, dry boughs must
    shed
  That nearer heaven the living ones may
    climb;
  The false must fail, though from our shores
    of time
The old lament be heard, — "Great Pan is
    dead!"
That wail is Error's, from his high place
    hurled;
  This sharp recoil is Evil undertrod;
  Our time's unrest, an angel sent of God
Troubling with life the waters of the world.
Even as they list the winds of the Spirit
    blow
  To turn or break our century-rusted vanes;
  Sands shift and waste; the rock alone
    remains

Where, led of Heaven, the strong tides come
    and go,
And storm-clouds, rent by thunderbolt and
    wind,
Leave, free of mist, the permanent stars be-
    hind.

Therefore I trust, although to outward sense
    Both true and false seem shaken; I will
    hold
    With newer light my reverence for the old,
And calmly wait the births of Providence.
No gain is lost; the clear-eyed saints look
    down
    Untroubled on the wreck of schemes and
    creeds;
    Love yet remains, its rosary of good deeds
Counting in task-field and o'er peopled town;
Truth has charmed life; the Inward Word
    survives,
    And, day by day, its revelation brings;
    Faith, hope, and charity, whatsoever things

Which cannot be shaken, stand.   Still holy
    lives
Reveal the Christ of whom the letter told,
And the new gospel verifies the old.

THE WOOD GIANT.

From Alton Bay to Sandwich Dome,
  From Mad to Saco river,
For patriarchs of the primal wood
  We sought with vain endeavor.

And then we said: " The giants old
  Are lost beyond retrieval;
This pigmy growth the axe has spared
  Is not the wood primeval.

" Look where we will o'er vale and hill,
  How idle are our searches
For broad-girthed maples, wide-limbed oaks,
  Centennial pines and birches !

" Their tortured limbs the axe and saw
  Have changed to beams and trestles;

They rest in walls, they float on seas,
    They rot in sunken vessels.

" This shorn and wasted mountain land
    Of underbrush and boulder, —
Who thinks to see its full-grown tree
    Must live a century older."

At last to us a woodland path,
    To open sunset leading,
Revealed the Anakim of pines
    Our wildest wish exceeding.

Alone, the level sun before;
    Below, the lake's green islands;
Beyond, in misty distance dim,
    The rugged Northern Highlands.

Dark Titan on his Sunset Hill
    Of time and change defiant!
How dwarfed the common woodland seemed,
    Before the old-time giant!

What marvel that, in simpler days
  Of the world's early childhood,
Men crowned with garlands, gifts, and praise
  Such monarchs of the wild-wood?

That Tyrian maids with flower and song
  Danced through the hill grove's spaces,
And hoary-bearded Druids found
  In woods their holy places?

With somewhat of that Pagan awe
  With Christian reverence blending,
We saw our pine-tree's mighty arms
  Above our heads extending.

We heard his needles' mystic rune,
 Now rising, and now dying,
As erst Dodona's priestess heard
  The oak leaves prophesying.

Was it the half-unconscious moan
  Of one apart and mateless,

The weariness of unshared power,
　The loneliness of greatness?

O dawns and sunsets, lend to him
　Your beauty and your wonder!
Blithe sparrow, sing thy summer song
　His solemn shadow under!

Play lightly on his slender keys,
　O wind of summer, waking
For hills like these the sound of seas
　On far-off beaches breaking!

And let the eagle and the crow
　Find shelter in his branches,
When winds shake down his winter snow
　In silver avalanches.

The brave are braver for their cheer,
　The strongest need assurance,
The sigh of longing makes not less
　The lesson of endurance.

THE HOMESTEAD.

AGAINST the wooded hills it stands,
  Ghost of a dead home, staring through
Its broken lights on wasted lands
  Where old-time harvests grew.

Unploughed, unsown, by scythe unshorn,
  The poor, forsaken farm-fields lie,
Once rich and rife with golden corn
  And pale green breadths of rye.

Of healthful herb and flower bereft,
  The garden plot no housewife keeps;
Through weeds and tangle only left,
  The snake, its tenant, creeps.

A lilac spray, once blossom-clad,
  Sways bare before the empty rooms;

Beside the roofless porch a sad
  Pathetic red rose blooms.

His track, in mould and dust of drouth,
  On floor and hearth the squirrel leaves,
And in the fireless chimney's mouth
  His web the spider weaves.

The leaning barn, about to fall,
  Resounds no more on husking eves;
No cattle low in yard or stall,
  No thresher beats his sheaves.

So sad, so drear! It seems almost
  Some haunting Presence makes its sign;
That down yon shadowy lane some ghost
  Might drive his spectral kine!

O home so desolate and lorn!
  Did all thy memories die with thee?
Were any wed, were any born,
  Beneath this low roof-tree?

Whose axe the wall of forest broke,
   And let the waiting sunshine through?
What good-wife sent the earliest smoke
   Up the great chimney flue?

Did rustic lovers hither come?
   Did maidens, swaying back and forth
In rhythmic grace, at wheel and loom,
   Make light their toil with mirth?

Did child feet patter on the stair?
   Did boyhood frolic in the snow?
Did gray age, in her elbow chair,
   Knit, rocking to and fro?

The murmuring brook, the sighing breeze,
   The pine's slow whisper, cannot tell;
Low mounds beneath the hemlock-trees
   Keep the home secrets well.

Cease, mother-land, to fondly boast
   Of sons far off who strive and thrive,

Forgetful that each swarming host
    Must leave an emptier hive!

O wanderers from ancestral soil,
    Leave noisome mill and chaffering store;
Gird up your loins for sturdier toil,
    And build the home once more!

Come back to bayberry-scented slopes,
    And fragrant fern, and ground-mat vine;
Breathe airs blown over holt and copse
    Sweet with black birch and pine.

What matter if the gains are small
    That life's essential wants supply?
Your homestead's title gives you all
    That idle wealth can buy.

All that the many-dollared crave,
    The brick-walled slaves of Change and mart,
Lawns, trees, fresh air, and flowers, you have,
    More dear for lack of art.

Your own sole masters, freedom-willed,
  With none to bid you go or stay,
Till the old fields your fathers tilled,
  As manly men as they!

With skill that spares your toiling hands,
  And chemic aid that science brings,
Reclaim the waste and outworn lands,
  And reign thereon as kings!

BIRCHBROOK MILL.

A NOTELESS stream, the Birchbrook runs
   Beneath its leaning trees;
That low, soft ripple is its own,
   That dull roar is the sea's.

Of human signs it sees alone
   The distant church spire's tip,
And, ghost-like, on a blank of gray,
   The white sail of a ship.

No more a toiler at the wheel,
   It wanders at its will;
Nor dam nor pond is left to tell
   Where once was Birchbrook mill.

The timbers of that mill have fed
   Long since a farmer's fires;

His doorsteps are the stones that ground
    The harvest of his sires.

Man trespassed here ; but. Nature lost
    No right of her domain ;
She waited, and she brought the old
    Wild beauty back again.

By day the sunlight through the leaves
    Falls on its moist, green sod,
And wakes the violet bloom of spring
    And autumn's golden-rod.

Its birches whisper to the wind,
    The swallow dips her wings
In the cool spray, and on its banks
    The gray song-sparrow sings.

But from it, when the dark night falls,
    The school-girl shrinks with dread ;
The farmer, home-bound from his fields,
    Goes by with quickened tread.

They dare not pause to hear the grind
  Of shadowy stone on stone;
The plashing of a water-wheel
  Where wheel there now is none.

Has not a cry of pain been heard
  Above the clattering mill?
The pawing of an unseen horse,
  Who waits his mistress still?

Yet never to the listener's eye
  Has sight confirmed the sound;
A wavering birch line marks alone
  The vacant pasture ground.

No ghostly arms fling up to heaven
  The agony of prayer;
No spectral steed impatient shakes
  His white mane on the air.

The meaning of that common dread
  No tongue has fitly told;

The secret of the dark surmise
The brook and birches hold.

What nameless horror of the past
Broods here forever more?
What ghost his unforgiven sin
Is grinding o'er and o'er?

Does, then, immortal memory play
The actor's tragic part,
Rehearsals of a mortal life
And unveiled human heart?

God's pity spare a guilty soul
That drama of its ill,
And let the scenic curtain fall
On Birchbrook's haunted mill!

HOW THE ROBIN CAME.

AN ALGONQUIN LEGEND.

HAPPY young friends, sit by me,
Under May's blown apple-tree,
While these home-birds in and out
Through the blossoms flit about.
Hear a story, strange and old,
By the wild red Indians told,
How the robin came to be:

Once a great chief left his son, —
Well-beloved, his only one, —
When the boy was well-nigh grown,
In the trial-lodge alone.
Left for tortures long and slow
Youths like him must undergo,
Who their pride of manhood test,
Lacking water, food, and rest.

3

Seven days the fast he kept,
Seven nights he never slept.
Then the young boy, wrung with pain,
Weak from nature's overstrain,
Faltering, moaned a low complaint:
"Spare me, father, for I faint!"
But the chieftain, haughty-eyed,
Hid his pity in his pride.
"You shall be a hunter good,
Knowing never lack of food;
You shall be a warrior great,
Wise as fox and strong as bear;
Many scalps your belt shall wear,
If with patient heart you wait
Bravely till your task is done.
Better you should starving die
Than that boy and squaw should cry
Shame upon your father's son!"

When next morn the sun's first rays
Glistened on the hemlock sprays,
Straight that lodge the old chief sought,

And boiled samp and moose meat brought.
" Rise and eat, my son ! " he said.
Lo, he found the poor boy dead !

As with grief his grave they made,
And his bow beside him laid,
Pipe, and knife, and wampum-braid,
On the lodge-top overhead,
Preening smooth its breast of red
And the brown coat that it wore,
Sat a bird, unknown before.
And as if with human tongue,
" Mourn me not," it said, or sung ;
" I, a bird, am still your son,
Happier than if hunter fleet,
Or a brave, before your feet
Laying scalps in battle won.
Friend of man, my song shall cheer
Lodge and corn-land ; hovering near,
To each wigwam I shall bring
Tidings of the coming spring ;
Every child my voice shall know

In the moon of melting snow,
When the maple's red bud swells,
And the wind-flower lifts its bells.
As their fond companion
Men shall henceforth own your son,
And my song shall testify
That of human kin am I."

Thus the Indian legend saith
How, at first, the robin came
With a sweeter life from death,
Bird for boy, and still the same.
If my young friends doubt that this
Is the robin's genesis,
Not in vain is still the myth
If a truth be found therewith:
Unto gentleness belong
Gifts unknown to pride and wrong;
Happier far than hate is praise, —
He who sings than he who slays.

SWEET FERN.

THE subtle power in perfume found
  Nor priest nor sibyl vainly learned;
On Grecian shrine or Aztec mound
  No censer idly burned.

That power the old-time worships knew,
  The Corybantes' frenzied dance,
The Pythian priestess swooning through
  The wonderland of trance.

And Nature holds, in wood and field,
  Her thousand sunlit censers still;
To spells of flower and shrub we yield
  Against or with our will.

I climbed a hill path strange and new
  With slow feet, pausing at each turn;

A sudden waft of west wind blew
  The breath of the sweet fern.

That fragrance from my vision swept
  The alien landscape; in its stead,
Up fairer hills of youth I stepped,
  As light of heart as tread.

I saw my boyhood's lakelet shine
  Once more through rifts of woodland shade;
I knew my river's winding line
  By morning mist betrayed.

With me June's freshness, lapsing brook,
  Murmurs of leaf and bee, the call
Of birds, and one in voice and look
  In keeping with them all.

A fern beside the way we went
  She plucked, and, smiling, held it up,
While from her hand the wild, sweet scent
  I drank as from a cup.

O potent witchery of smell!
   The dust-dry leaves to life return,
And she who plucked them owns the spell
   And lifts her ghostly fern.

Or sense or spirit? Who shall say
   What touch the chord of memory thrills?
It passed, and left the August day
   Ablaze on lonely hills.

BANISHED FROM MASSACHUSETTS.

1660.

ON A PAINTING BY E. A. ABBEY.

OVER the threshold of his pleasant home
  Set in green clearings passed the exiled
      Friend,
  In simple trust, misdoubting not the end.
"Dear heart of mine!" he said, "the time
      has come
To trust the Lord for shelter." One long
      gaze
  The good wife turned on each familiar
      thing,—
  The lowing kine, the orchard blossoming,
The open door that showed the hearth-fire's
      blaze, —
And calmly answered, "Yes, He will provide."

Silent and slow they crossed the homestead's
bound,

Lingering the longest by their child's grave-
mound.

"Move on, or stay and hang!" the sheriff
cried.

They left behind them more than home or
land,

And set sad faces to an alien strand.

Safer with winds and waves than human
wrath,

With ravening wolves than those whose zeal
for God

Was cruelty to man, the exiles trod

Drear leagues of forest without guide or path,

Or launching frail boats on the uncharted sea,

Round storm-vexed capes, whose teeth of
granite ground

The waves to foam, their perilous way they
wound,

Enduring all things so their souls were free.

Oh, true confessors, shaming them who did
  Anew the wrong their Pilgrim Fathers bore!
  For you the Mayflower spread her sail once
    more,
Freighted with souls, to all that duty bid
Faithful as they who sought an unknown
    land,
O'er wintry seas, from Holland's Hook of
    Sand!

So from his lost home to the darkening
    main,
  Bodeful of storm, stout Macey held his
    way,
  And, when the green shore blended with
    the gray,
His poor wife moaned: "Let us turn back
    again."
"Nay, woman, weak of faith, kneel down,"
    said he,
  "And say thy prayers: the Lord himself
    will steer;

And led by Him, nor man nor devils I
  fear ! " [1]
So the gray Southwicks, from a rainy sea,
Saw, far and faint, the loom of land, and
  gave
With feeble voices thanks for friendly
  ground
Whereon to rest their weary feet, and found
A peaceful death-bed and a quiet grave
Where, ocean-walled, and wiser than his age,
The lord of Shelter scorned the bigot's rage.

Aquidneck's isle, Nantucket's lonely shores,
  And Indian-haunted Narragansett saw
  The way-worn travellers round their camp-
    fire draw,
Or heard the plashing of their weary oars.

---

[1] " He [Macey] shook the dust from off his feet, and departed with all
his worldly goods and his family. He encountered a severe storm, and
his wife, influenced by some omens of disaster, besought him to put back.
He told her not to fear, for his faith was perfect. But she entreated him
again. Then the spirit that impelled him broke forth : ' Woman, go be-
low and seek thy God. I fear not the witches on earth, or the devils in
hell ! ' " — *Life of Robert Pike*, page 55.

And every place whereon they rested grew
  Happier for pure and gracious womanhood,
  And men whose names for stainless honor
    stood,
Founders of States and rulers wise and true.
The Muse of history yet shall make amends
  To those who freedom, peace, and justice
    taught,
  Beyond their dark age led the van of
    thought,
And left unforfeited the name of Friends.
Oh mother State, how foiled was thy design!
The gain was theirs, the loss alone was thine.

THE TWO ELIZABETHS.

Read at the unveiling of the bust of Elizabeth Fry at the Friends' School, Providence, R. I.

A. D. 1209.

AMIDST Thuringia's wooded hills she dwelt,
 A high-born princess, servant of the poor,
Sweetening with gracious words the food she
  dealt
 To starving throngs at Wartburg's blazoned
  door.

A blinded zealot held her soul in chains,
 Cramped the sweet nature that he could
  not kill,
Scarred her fair body with his penance-pains,
 And gauged her conscience by his narrow will.

God gave her gifts of beauty and of grace,
 With fast and vigil she denied them all;

Unquestioning, with sad, pathetic face,
　She followed meekly at her stern guide's
　　call.

So drooped and died her home-blown rose of
　　bliss
　In the chill rigor of a discipline
That turned her fond lips from her children's
　　kiss,
　And made her joy of motherhood a sin.

To their sad level by compassion led,
　One with the low and vile herself she
　　made,
While thankless misery mocked the hand that
　　fed,
　And laughed to scorn her piteous masque-
　　rade.

But still, with patience that outwearied hate,
　She gave her all while yet she had to
　　give;

And then her empty hands, importunate,
  In prayer she lifted that the poor might
    live.

Sore pressed by grief, and wrongs more hard
    to bear,
  And dwarfed and stifled by a harsh con-
    trol,
She kept life fragrant with good deeds and
    prayer,
  And fresh and pure the white flower of her
    soul.

Death found her busy at her task: one word
  Alone she uttered as she paused to die,
"Silence!" — then listened even as one who
    heard
  With song and wing the angels drawing
    nigh!

Now Fra Angelico's roses fill her hands,
  And, on Murillo's canvas, Want and Pain

Kneel at her feet.　Her marble image stands
　　Worshipped and crowned in Marburg's holy
　　　　fane.

Yea, wheresoe'er her Church its cross uprears,
　　Wide as the world her story still is told;
In manhood's reverence, woman's prayers and
　　　　tears,
　　She lives again whose grave is centuries old.

And still, despite the weakness or the blame
　　Of blind submission to the blind, she hath
A tender place in hearts of every name,
　　And more than Rome owns Saint Elizabeth!

A. D. 1780.

Slow ages passed: and lo! another came,
　　An English matron, in whose simple faith
Nor priestly rule nor ritual had claim,
　　A plain, uncanonized Elizabeth.

No sackcloth robe, nor ashen-sprinkled hair,
　　Nor wasting fast, nor scourge, nor vigil long,

Marred her calm presence. God had made
    her fair,
  And she could do His goodly work no wrong.

Their yoke is easy and their burden light
  Whose sole confessor is the Christ of God;
Her quiet trust and faith transcending sight
  Smoothed to her feet the difficult paths she
    trod.

And there she walked, as duty bade her go,
  Safe and unsullied as a cloistered nun,
Shamed with her plainness Fashion's gaudy
    show,
  And overcame the world she did not shun.

In Earlham's bowers, in Plashet's liberal hall,
  In the great city's restless crowd and din,
Her ear was open to the Master's call,
  And knew the summons of His voice within.

Tender as mother, beautiful as wife,
  Amidst the throngs of prisoned crime she
    stood,

In modest raiment faultless as her life,
  The type of England's worthiest woman-
    hood !

To melt the hearts that harshness turned to
    stone
  The sweet persuasion of her lips sufficed,
And guilt, which only hate and fear had
    known,
  Saw in her own the pitying love of Christ.

So wheresoe'er the guiding Spirit went
  She followed, finding every prison cell
It opened for her sacred as a tent
  Pitched by Gennesaret or by Jacob's well.

And Pride and Fashion felt her strong ap-
    peal,
  And priest and ruler marvelled as they
    saw
How hand in hand went wisdom with her
    zeal,
  And woman's pity kept the bounds of law.

She rests in God's peace; but her memory
    stirs
The air of earth as with an angel's wings,
And warms and moves the hearts of men like
    hers,
    The sainted daughter of Hungarian kings.

United now, the Briton and the Hun,
    Each, in her own time, faithful unto death,
Live sister souls! in name and spirit one,
    Thuringia's saint and our Elizabeth!

THE REUNION.

Read September 10, 1885, to the surviving students of Haverhill Academy in 1827-28.

THE gulf of seven and fifty years
    We stretch our welcoming hands across;
    The distance but a pebble's toss
Between us and our youth appears.

For in life's school we linger on
    The remnant of a once full list;
    Conning our lessons, undismissed,
With faces to the setting sun.

And some have gone the unknown way,
    And some await the call to rest;
    Who knoweth whether it is best
For those who went or those who stay?

And yet despite of loss and ill,
   If faith and love and hope remain,
   Our length of days is not in vain,
And life is well worth living still.

Still to a gracious Providence
   The thanks of grateful hearts are due,
   For blessings when our lives were new,
For all the good vouchsafed us since.

The pain that spared us sorer hurt,
   The wish denied, the purpose crossed,
   And pleasure's fond occasions lost,
Were mercies to our small desert.

'T is something that we wander back,
   Gray pilgrims, to our ancient ways,
   And tender memories of old days
Walk with us by the Merrimac;

That even in life's afternoon
   A sense of youth comes back again,

As through this cool September rain
The still green woodlands dream of June.

The eyes grown dim to present things
    Have keener sight for by-gone years,
    And sweet and clear, in deafening ears,
The bird that sang at morning sings.

Dear comrades, scattered wide and far,
    Send from their homes their kindly word,
    And dearer ones, unseen, unheard,
Smile on us from some heavenly star.

For life and death with God are one,
    Unchanged by seeming change His care
    And love are round us here and there;
He breaks no thread His hand has spun.

Soul touches soul, the muster roll
    Of life eternal has no gaps;
    And after half a century's lapse
Our school-day ranks are closed and whole.

Hail and farewell! We go our way;
  Where shadows end, we trust in light;
  The star that ushers in the night
Is herald also of the day!

REQUITAL.

As Islam's Prophet, when his last day drew
  Nigh to its close, besought all men to say
  Whom he had wronged, to whom he then
    should pay
A debt forgotten, or for pardon sue,
And, through the silence of his weeping
  friends,
  A strange voice cried : "Thou owest me a
    debt,"
"Allah be praised!" he answered. "Even yet
He gives me power to make to thee amends.
Oh, friend! I thank thee for thy timely word."
  So runs the tale. Its lesson all may heed,
  For all have sinned in thought, or word, or
    deed,

Or, like the Prophet, through neglect have
    erred.

All need forgiveness, all have debts to pay
Ere the night cometh, while it still is day.

THE LIGHT THAT IS FELT.

A TENDER child of summers three,
  Seeking her little bed at night,
Paused on the dark stair timidly.
"Oh, mother! Take my hand," said she,
  "And then the dark will all be light."

We older children grope our way
  From dark behind to dark before;
And only when our hands we lay,
Dear Lord, in Thine, the night is day,
  And there is darkness nevermore.

Reach downward to the sunless days
  Wherein our guides are blind as we,
And faith is small and hope delays;
Take Thou the hands of prayer we raise,
  And let us feel the light of Thee!

THE TWO LOVES.

Smoothing soft the nestling head
Of a maiden fancy-led,
Thus a grave-eyed woman said:

"Richest gifts are those we make,
Dearer than the love we take
That we give for love's own sake.

"Well I know the heart's unrest;
Mine has been the common quest
To be loved and therefore blest.

"Favors undeserved were mine;
At my feet as on a shrine
Love has laid its gifts divine.

"Sweet the offerings seemed, and yet
With their sweetness came regret,
And a sense of unpaid debt.

" Heart of mine unsatisfied,
 Was it vanity or pride
 That a deeper joy denied ?

" Hands that ope but to receive
 Empty close; they only live
 Richly who can richly give.

" Still," she sighed, with moistening eyes,
" Love is sweet in any guise ;
 But its best is sacrifice !

" He who, giving, does not crave
 Likest is to Him who gave
 Life itself the loved to save.

" Love, that self-forgetful gives,
 Sows surprise of ripened sheaves,
 Late or soon its own receives."

AN EASTER FLOWER GIFT.

O DEAREST bloom the seasons know,
Flowers of the Resurrection blow,
   Our hope and faith restore ;
And through the bitterness of death
And loss and sorrow, breathe a breath
   Of life forevermore !

The thought of Love Immortal blends
With fond remembrances of friends ;
   In you, O sacred flowers,
By human love made doubly sweet,
The heavenly and the earthly meet,
   The heart of Christ and ours !

MULFORD.

AUTHOR OF "THE NATION". AND "THE REPUBLIC
OF GOD."

UNNOTED as the setting of a star
    He passed; and sect and party scarcely
      knew
    When from their midst a sage and seer with-
      drew
To fitter audience, where the great dead are
In God's republic of the heart and mind,
Leaving no purer, nobler soul behind.

AN ARTIST OF THE BEAUTIFUL.

G. F.

HAUNTED of Beauty, like the marvellous
    youth
Who sang Saint Agnes' Eve! How passing
    fair
Her shapes took color in thy homestead air!
How on thy canvas even her dreams were
    truth!
Magician! who from commonest elements
Called up divine ideals, clothed upon
By mystic lights soft blending into one
Womanly grace and child-like innocence.
Teacher! thy lesson was not given in vain.
Beauty is goodness; ugliness is sin;
Art's place is sacred: nothing foul therein
May crawl or tread with bestial feet profane.
If rightly choosing is the painter's test,
Thy choice, O master, ever was the best.

HYMNS OF THE BRAHMO SOMAJ.[1]

I.

THE mercy, O Eternal One!
　By man unmeasured yet,
In joy or grief, in shade or sun,
　I never will forget.
I give the whole, and not a part,
　Of all Thou gavest me;
My goods, my life, my soul and heart,
　I yield them all to Thee!

II.

We fast and plead, we weep and pray,
　From morning until even;

---

[1] I have attempted this paraphrase of the Hymns of the Brahmo Somaj of India, as I find them in Mozoomdar's account of the devotional exercises of that remarkable religious development which has attracted far less attention and sympathy from the Christian world than it deserves, as a fresh revelation of the direct action of the Divine Spirit upon the human heart.

We feel to find the holy way,
  We knock at the gate of heaven!
And when in silent awe we wait,
  And word and sign forbear,
The hinges of the golden gate
  Move, soundless, to our prayer!
Who hears the eternal harmonies
  Can heed no outward word;
Blind to all else is he who sees
  The vision of the Lord!

III.

O soul, be patient, restrain thy tears,
  Have hope, and not despair;
As a tender mother heareth her child
  God hears the penitent prayer.
And not forever shall grief be thine;
  On the Heavenly Mother's breast,
Washed clean and white in the waters of joy
  Shall His seeking child find rest.

Console thyself with His word of grace,
   And cease thy wail of woe,
For His mercy never an equal hath,
   And His love no bounds can know.
Lean close unto Him in faith and hope;
   How many like thee have found
In Him a shelter and home of peace,
   By His mercy compassed round!
There, safe from sin and the sorrow it brings,
   They sing their grateful psalms,
And rest, at noon, by the wells of God,
   In the shade of His holy palms!

www.ingramcontent.com/pod-product-compliance
Lightning Source LLC
Chambersburg PA
CBHW021518090426
42739CB00007B/674